Thomas Jefferson

BY XINA M. UHL

The Child's World®
childsworld.com

Published by The Child's World®
1980 Lookout Drive • Mankato, MN 56003-1705
800-599-READ • www.childsworld.com

Acknowledgments
The Child's World®: Mary Swensen, Publishing Director
Red Line Editorial: Editorial direction and production
The Design Lab: Design

Photographs ©: Corbis, cover, 1, 18; Bettmann/Corbis, 4;
John Trumbull, 7; GraphicaArtis/Corbis, 8; Chris Pecoraro/
iStockphoto, 11; Alfred Jones/Library of Congress, 12; Everett
Historical/Shutterstock Images, 14; iStockphoto, 17; ©
Thomas Jefferson Foundation at Monticello, 21

ISBN 9781503808775
LCCN 2015958437

Printed in the United States of America
Mankato, MN
June, 2016
PA02303

ABOUT THE AUTHOR

Xina M. Uhl loves history, hiking, travel, and pizza. She lives in southern California with her family and a bunch of dogs.

Table of Contents

★ ★ ★

Jefferson was a talented writer.

CHAPTER ONE

Declaring Independence

★ ★ ★

In May 1776, Thomas Jefferson left his home in Virginia. A week later, he came to Philadelphia, Pennsylvania. He and other American leaders had a meeting. It was called the Second Continental Congress.

The American **colonies** were at war with England. England wanted to keep ruling the colonies. Congress wanted the colonies to be free.

Jefferson spoke little at the meetings. But he had a talent for writing. Soon, it was time to write about Congress's beliefs. A document would say that the colonies were free. The other members of Congress asked Jefferson to write the first **draft**.

Jefferson did not want the job. He thought John Adams should write it. Adams was also in Congress.

Adams did not agree. He liked Jefferson's way with words. So Adams said, "You can write ten times better than I can."

Jefferson thought about it. He said, "Well, if you are decided, I will do as well as I can."

He worked for two and a half weeks. His draft said many things. One was that all men had rights. Some of these rights were to "Life, Liberty and the pursuit of Happiness." Another was that England would no longer rule the colonies. King George III

Jefferson gave his first draft of the Declaration of Independence to Congress.

had cut off the colonies' trade. He had **taxed** them. The **colonists** had no say in these taxes. Now, laws would not come from the king. They would come from the people.

Jefferson sent the document to Congress in late June. Congress made some changes. On July 4, 1776, leaders from 12 colonies signed it. It was called the Declaration of Independence.

With this document, Jefferson had helped start a new country. That country became the United States of America.

Jefferson attended the College of William and Mary.

CHAPTER TWO

The Early Years

★ ★ ★

Thomas Jefferson was born on April 13, 1743. His father was a wealthy planter. His mother came from a well-known family. They lived in Virginia. His father died in 1757. He gave his son his land. It was a large estate. Jefferson was 14 years old. He took charge of it when he turned 21.

Jefferson went to college young. He was only 17 years old. He attended the College of William and Mary. Two years later, he studied law. He became a lawyer. The job took him many places in his state.

At age 26, he began a big task. He built a home on his land. Its name was Monticello. He worked on it for 15 years. The house was big and beautiful. It had 43 rooms! The house sat on a large plot of land. Pretty gardens grew there.

Jefferson did not like slavery. But he kept his own slaves. So did many other colonists. Slaves cooked his meals. They worked his farm. They lived in cabins nearby.

In 1765, Jefferson heard Patrick Henry speak. Henry was a lawyer. He did not want to pay taxes to the king. Jefferson agreed. He wanted to change the laws. In 1769, he entered **politics**. He joined the House of Burgesses. This was the name of Virginia's government.

Jefferson built his home, Monticello, in Virginia.

Patrick Henry (right) was an influential speaker.

Jefferson married Martha Skelton on January 1, 1772. They were happy together. They started a family.

CHAPTER THREE

Shaping a Country

★ ★ ★

Jefferson worked in the House of Burgesses for five years. He helped form a **committee**. It opposed British rule. He also wrote an **essay**. It said that the king did not let Virginia make its own laws. The king kept the colony from ending slavery. But Jefferson said that was illegal. Many people in Virginia liked Jefferson's ideas. Lawmakers began to like him. In 1775, America started fighting England. The colonies wanted to be free. In 1776, the Second Continental Congress had Jefferson write the Declaration of Independence.

Jefferson helped make the American money system we use today.

In 1776, the name of the House of Burgesses changed. Now, Jefferson was part of the Virginia House of Delegates. He wrote a bill. It kept laws from being made about religions. He also tried to create free schools. Going to school cost money in the 1700s.

Jefferson changed jobs. He became Virginia's **governor**. Then, the Second Continental Congress took a new name. They were now the Confederation Congress. Jefferson joined them. He made a new American money system. Each colony had its own money. This confused people. They wanted money to be the same in all colonies. Jefferson had a new idea. He would count money in tens. Ten dimes would make up one dollar. This is called the **decimal system**. The United States still uses this money system today.

In 1783, America won the war with England. America was free. In 1785, Jefferson went to France. He was a **diplomat** there. While he was gone, a group of men at home had a task. They wrote the U.S. Constitution. It created the U.S. government. Jefferson helped these men. He wrote them letters from France. He wanted to add a bill of rights. This bill would protect many freedoms. One freedom was freedom of speech. This is the right to say what one wants.

In 1790, George Washington became president. He knew that Jefferson was a good leader. So he gave Jefferson a new role. Now, Jefferson was the secretary of state. He was in charge of American diplomats. He tried to help America and France work together. He held this job until 1793.

Jefferson helped write the U.S. Constitution.

Jefferson (left) signed for the purchase of the Louisiana Territory from France.

CHAPTER FOUR

Presidency and Beyond

★ ★ ★

The third presidential **election** was in 1796. John Adams won. Jefferson came in second. He became vice president. In 1800, Jefferson ran for president again. He won.

In 1803, the country doubled in size. The United States bought land from France. It was called the Louisiana Territory.

Jefferson was a popular president. In 1804, he was reelected. England and France were at war. They said

America should join them. The British took American sailors to fight as British sailors. Jefferson did not want war. He tried to fix the problem. He made American ships stay in American ports. They would be safe from the British there. But Americans did not like that. They could not sell goods to England.

Jefferson left office in 1809. Then, he went home. He read books. He wrote letters. He started a university. He created a special bookstand. It turned around.

In 1814, a fire burned many books in the Library of Congress. Jefferson sold 6,487 of his books to Congress the next year. The books replaced the burned ones.

He still worried about slavery. He said it would destroy the country. But he never freed his own slaves.

On July 4, 1826, the United States turned 50 years old. The nation celebrated. But Jefferson had been sick. He died on the country's birthday. He was buried at his home.

Few people did as much for America as Jefferson did. He helped the country break free of England. His work shaped America's laws. That is why Americans still remember him today.

1740

← **April 13, 1743** Thomas Jefferson is born.

← **1767** Jefferson begins practicing law.

← **1769** Jefferson starts building Monticello.

← **January 1, 1772** Jefferson marries Martha Skelton.

← **June 10, 1776** Jefferson begins writing the Declaration of Independence.

← **1783** Jefferson is elected to Congress.

← **1790** Jefferson begins his role as secretary of state.

← **1797** Jefferson becomes vice president.

← **March 4, 1801** Jefferson becomes president.

← **1809** Jefferson retires from politics.

← **1815** The Library of Congress buys thousands of Jefferson's books.

← **July 4, 1826** Jefferson dies.

1830

colonies (KOL-uh-nees) Colonies are large areas of land that are ruled by another country. The American colonies wanted freedom from Britain.

colonists (KOL-uh-nists) Colonists are people who live on land that is starting to be settled. England taxed American colonists.

committee (kuh-MIT-ee) A group of people who have a task is called a committee. Jefferson joined a committee to write a statement of beliefs.

decimal system (DES-i-mal SIS-tum) A decimal system is a way to group units based on the number ten. It was Jefferson's idea to base American money on the decimal system.

diplomat (DIP-lo-mat) A diplomat is a person who is skilled at helping two countries work together. Thomas Jefferson was a diplomat to France.

draft (DRAFT) An early version from which a finished product will be produced is known as a draft. Jefferson wrote the first draft of the Declaration of Independence.

election (i-LEK-shun) An election is when people choose a leader by voting. Jefferson ran in the third presidential election, but lost.

essay (EHS-ay) A writing that gives an opinion about some subject is an essay. Jefferson wrote an essay about religion and government.

governor (GUV-uh-ner) A governor is the head of a state or colony. Jefferson served as governor of Virginia.

politics (POL-uh-tiks) Politics are activities to gain or hold onto power in government. Jefferson worked in politics for 40 years.

taxed (TAKST) When people are taxed, they have to pay money to the government. The king of England taxed the colonists.

In the Library

Collard, Sneed B. III. *Thomas Jefferson: Let Freedom Ring!*
New York: Marshall Cavendish Benchmark, 2009.

Harness, Cheryl. *Thomas Jefferson.* Washington, DC:
National Geographic, 2007.

Kalman, Maira. *Thomas Jefferson; Life, Liberty and the Pursuit
of Everything.* New York: Nancy Paulsen Books, 2014.

On the Web

Visit our Web site for links about Thomas Jefferson:
childsworld.com/links

*Note to Parents, Teachers, and Librarians: We routinely verify our Web links to make
sure they are safe and active sites. So encourage your readers to check them out!*

INDEX